Model Organism

Robert S. Pesich

Five Oaks Press
FIVE-OAKS-PRESS.COM

Copyright ©2017 Robert S. Pesich
All rights reserved. First print edition.

Five Oaks Press
Newburgh, NY 12550
five-oaks-press.com
editor@five-oaks-press.com

ISBN: 978-1-944355-24-1

Cover & Book Design: Lynn Houston

Printed in the United States of America

CONTENTS

A Few Questions 7

A Window in the City 8

Heart Massage 9

NUDE Mouse 11

Cardiac Morphogenesis 13

Total Lunar Eclipse 15

Mice and Other Guests 17

Recommendation: Maggot Therapy for Wound Debridement 18

The *eyeless* Gene in *Drosophila melanogaster* 19

Xenopus laevis: African Clawed Frog 20

And What Will You Admit 22

To a Red-Tailed Hawk 23

Dressing Up In Down Times 25

Production of the Next, Safe Happies 26

The Stomach 27

Pet Shop 28

Arriving at the Dept. of Systems & Chemical Biology 29

A Quick Stop at the Natural Life Aquarium 30

Father & Son Q&A 31

Blasphemous Pilgrim 32

Kitchen Science No.7: Surface Tension 33

The 6 O'Clock Commute 34

Tissue Culture 35

Chinese Lanterns in a Shadowbox 36

The Envelope Has Something to Say 37

From a Dead Fox in a Suburban Backyard 38

For Sanja, Nikola and Anton

A Few Questions

Who says the wind and tree always argue,
that suspicion ripens the persimmon?

If this is true, how naked must water be
in order to enter the fruit?

But isn't everything in everything?

Why not listen to them tonight
as they undress themselves in the other.

Thank the persimmons, lanterns for cold hands,
while those on the ground ask us to kneel.

Yes, the dark bruise from the fall,
tender underside of the heart

earth suggesting we begin there,
sweet blossom of water for our lips.

A Window in the City

I was in the back, in the bathroom,
reading the Times on the toilet,
a small article under a yellow night-light
because the switch was blown:
"Old woman finds infant in dumpster,
revives him with songs."
It was then that I could hear
someone knocking on the neglected
window in the corner, above my face.
A small bird, dark as my eyes
returning to her chicks.
The nest wedged against the hinge
keeping the window open with its woven
mouth of mud, grass and tangled
cassette tape holding my voice,
a few words, a brief song, made useful.
Tiny ligature of a greater voice,
that brings me to the window.
Black back-alley, bricks,
dumpster and sour diesel.
The birds resting in my breath
while outside, someone shatters
a glass or a mirror
under a brief snow of blossoms
floating down from somewhere.

Heart Massage

The swift explodes into feathers
plunges over the field
then rises, in death
flying in the falcon's talons,
its life torn apart
to feed more life
and in secret.

You would not lament
this moment, growing it
as a song, a third heart
within your voice,
within your hands
which I still remember, love

their scent of fresh turned earth
even on the gurney in that ER.
Your body plowed
with wires and tubes,
the stray bullet in your side.

Your heart massaged
to nothing
at an altar of monitors.

Simply walking to work

And then
           And then

Still no sky in my dreams of you.

Still nothing when I hear your voice
and turn to see

and turn   to nothing
                                  god

NUDE Mouse

A nude mouse, hairless and wrinkled,
squats next to a storm drain,
pale patch of human skin
grafted to its bony back.
Nibbling something
shaped like my dreams.
Whatever it is, he keeps it,
scurries down into the darkness
to hide under scarlet leaves
and plastic garbage in the drainage
that flows to the sea
as I walk across the parking lot
to receive my diagnosis
from internal medicine.

Underneath the hospital,
generations of mice and rats
living in climate controlled cages
wait for the lights to go out.
They don't know the pencil
will often be used
to break their necks.

Who knows how this one managed
to escape, how long he'll live out here.
Mutant with hardly any immune system.
Skinny little body rooted for answers.

And who needs to be notified?
What does that human skin graft feel like?
Maybe hard and mostly numb,
burning at the borders,
pulling at everything as it fists.

Cardiac Morphogenesis

Physiology professors continue to announce
to their class, "Make a fist, your heart is that big."

The initials carved in the desktops, part of
the eternal addition, whisper their rebuttal,
"Just enough room for a splinter of metal."

The homework usually involves identification
of structure and function.

Exams follow. Multiple choice/fill-in.
Sometimes an essay question
concerning relationships:
> Describe the path of an impulse
> through the heart.
> How does one cell depolarize another?
> What is the quiescent period?
> What is heart block?

Very few ace this course. Most pass.

Subjects of conversation at the 30-year reunion
include the children, house, new career path,
last year's cruise on the Love Boat
to get away from it all while taking it all
with us. How time flies as we grow heavier.
A few words now about the old flame, nostalgia,
our sins of omission, turning to the arrhythmias,
that sudden heart attack,
the prolapse in our night's empty bed.

No mention was made about morphogenesis
in my class, how cells first form a primitive cardiac-tube, a tunnel.
Rhythmic contractions starting around day 23,
the cardiac-tube then undergoing
a rightward looping.

The beginning embedded in the end, the end embedded in the beginning. The mature heart, a circle whose perimeter is also described by the anti-fist. The wind in our lungs whispering, "Just enough room in there for a spark."

Total Lunar Eclipse

For months we forget about you
while your blue light tries to pry
through the bedroom blinds
to enter our dreams.

    *

Dark side of the moon, the unseen,
my teacher
also illuminated by the sun.

    *

Again you are the shape of a curved needle
for the wounds in my side
as I search for my country

    within my country

        year after year

absence and questions   the sutures

    secured and absorbed

    *

Once again we hit you,
this time with a Centaur rocket
in search of water among your craters.

    *

'67? Or was it '68? September
when they orbited the moon
secured in their Zond capsule
surviving reentry, splashdown.

Those two Russian
steppe tortoises
where are they now?
Nameless, those two. Let them
outlive me.

*

Quiet. Smoke
rising towards the moon
will also teach us
how to travel.

Mice and Other Guests

They wake us up at night.

They come and go as they please.

Running across the roof,
scratching in the attic.

The traps we set
only catch our sight.

You might see them
if you forget your face,
which fits nicely
in one of their footprints.

What we forget, they sow.
Seeds in every corner of our house.

The wind arrives, lowers itself swiftly
down the chimney to drink.

Invisible roots tap us for water.

Blossoming above us, fields of stars.

Recommendation: Maggot Therapy for Wound Debridement

What is it about the healthy
that these little buggers should desire instead
only the dying and the dead

for their sustenance in the wound,
the burned margins offering as much perhaps:
fragile connectives, essential

salts and sugars of our tissues,
blood and oblivions, their embraces
evidencing just out of sight.

The *eyeless* Gene in *Drosophila melanogaster*

Now we can fool with any gene
any sequence of nucleotides
even in the homeobox,
looking to mutants
to answer our questions.

Inducing the fly's *eyeless* gene
to express itself in the imaginal discs
results in ruby red eyes
growing on the antennae, legs and wings.

The little eyes in back of this one's head
stare at you as you approach
with stainless needles and knives
and a sterile vial for clues.
Pay better attention.

When the ether wears off, it flirts
then flies from the light of the stage
as if to say, I see better
in the dark and the dust.

No, as if to say the *I* is difficult to pin down,
how it evolved, where it's going.
The little joker escaping now, out the window,
nowhere and everywhere to be found.

Xenopus laevis: **African Clawed Frog**

Abandoned, likely by a scientist,
in Golden Gate Park just East
of the National Academy of Sciences.
The lily pond your new home
and with no natural predators
you flourish, ravenous
even against your own young.

Xenopus, show yourself
to the lovers and the children
before the Department of Fish & Game
arrive to eradicate you
with explosives.

Show how you hunt
whatever moves
including their fingers
and reflections
among the yellow lotus
as they throw coins
large as their eyes,
a wish
while trying to taste a petal.

If you claw my palm
I'll call it a sign
that you are naming us
according to a ruptured light.
The scar will remind me
during the coming droughts and firestorms
that the song can survive detonations,
living underground, consuming its own
shed skin with plans to return
with or without us.

And What Will You Admit

when the zero hour in your name
demands that grief be accompanied
by solitude and a yielding
to a current that removes you
from what you call home to a shoreline
where nothing more can be done
but let the birds and breaking
waves speak through the amalgams
they create from the useless and abandoned
how to find the secret colors
present in a halftoned landscape
not unlike the royal purple
gleaming in the dusty eyes
of their black feathers
focused on origin and horizon
present in every direction.

To a Red-Tailed Hawk

You chose the cinderblock wall for this kill.
The final stutter of hind legs in the squirrel,
head thrown back, belly split, mouth gaping.
I slow my breath,
hear the tear of tendon and muscle like paper
as you open the dark liver and scarlet lungs.
How you pierce the hot pleurae, gain
the last vital capacity
as if sky was not enough.
As if to demonstrate a tradition
between earth and sky, their trembling dance—
the wet stretch of peritoneum
between talon and beak.
How you claw the umber stomach out,
its mass of earth:
acorn-meat, acids, enzymes, mucus.

You drop the dollop to asphalt,
regard me with slight interest
as I consider the weight of my guts.
My anemic blood: tars, xylenes, cancer radicals.
The weight of my pelvic girdle,
heavy metals in bone.
I plod earth to this witness:

your cry, sudden flare of wings,
your grip of rigor.
How you rise in the perfect hollowness of bone
leaving me bent over
the small remains of intimidation:
bone, lymph, blood and
the beautiful dark song of stomach, glistening,
and the shadows they leave
slowly fading with time.

Dressing Up in Down Times

The tailor of faces
with clients in Congress
as well as your neighbor.
He understands your needs
even those for a new look
to reflect the new world order
and slowly falling sky.

Just looking at your hair,
he knows your number.
The chalk behind his ear,
bone from his mentor's index finger.

For a little extra
he'll solve your panic attacks,
line your picked pockets
with fresh turtle hearts.
They'll beat against your wrists
through the New Year.
He'll even throw in
a couple of shark teeth
necklaces for your kids.

Production of the Next, Safe Happies

Years after they privatized the reservoirs, rivers and lakes they finally
took even the mountain peaks, leaving us with nothing.

Our nothings mumble in abandoned schools.
Our nothings accompany us across empty fields
as we migrate now in search of our names.

Rumored to be durable and pliable,
a new-age psychoactive neo-material,
they returned to harvest our nothings.

Substrates for the synthesis of new therapeutics
marketed as the next, safe Happies,
users remember good-times they never had.

Although only a little better than placebos,
our new-and-improved nothings sell well
at their Costco, effecting a new normal,

the side-effects yet to be reported
as we migrate North in search of our disappeared, their names on watchlists

and school bulletin boards.

The Stomach

What we call our trawler does not stop at night. It continues to growl, hiss and pitch for the next catch, our search for something to love, good enough to eat. Everything processed below deck in half-light. The low-value ground, reformed into nostalgias named Medley, Chorus, Family-Pak. Word now often comes from corporate, software manufacturing taste.

Pet Shop

People are wandering the aisles
looking for a pet. I am there
in the back with the silence

attending the fish and stones
who know about the false
currency under our tongue.

Even the walking-sticks disappear
among the reeds. They know we are thieves,
having stolen the fruit, water, fire…

Our grandmothers are live
ash, long white braids of smoke
rising into the hole in the sky,

leaving unrecognized by our children,
who continue trying to catch
anything that moves.

No loitering. Do not touch.
You break, you pay.
When no one is looking

I offer my fingertips.
Gold surfaces from the dark,
lips, soft as an infant's ears.

All day and all night
people tapping the glass,
desire to see, to be seen.

Arriving at the Dept. of Systems & Chemical Biology

A hummingbird flies past our face just as we exit the elevator to the Department of Systems and Chemical Biology. He collides into the East window, turns, flies back down the hallway. Every door, closed. Flying back and forth who knows how long. He collides into the West and drops to the floor. A wing continues to unfold, fold. Doors open next to him. A young woman exits wearing a white lab coat and carrying a small black computer. She stops, glances at the body then retreats. We are still lost. Here, the room numbers are all even. We're looking for 701. The same door opens. She reappears wearing sky-blue nitrile gloves. She picks up the bird for the tail, drops it in a red biohazard bag that expands, contracts as she seals it for the incinerator.

A Quick Stop at the Natural Life Aquarium

They also sell snakes, lizards and parakeets.
We visit once in awhile. My son is three now
and trying to tap into every window
while I listen to a woman on the other side
among the freshwater tanks
explaining to her friend,
When we finally separated, I changed my mind
and got my son a pet, zebrafish,
simple, a big bowl with rocks
and a decrepit castle.
My son is already there, tapping the glass
the fish zig zagging to his delight.
They are native to the Ganges
and in streams and stagnant bodies
    of water in ditches.
And I want to correct her.
Yes, they are simple.
One for $1.99, three for $4
and you can also cut them slightly
at home in the kitchen.
Squeeze out the two-chambered heart.
Chop off a chunk, at its apex,
staunch the bleeding and push it back in.
I keep telling myself even now
eight out of ten make it and go on
to regenerate what was amputated
through a series of clots.
Scarring vs. regeneration not understood.
The first full moon will see a new heart wall.
The next full moon will see the heart grown
back to its previous form
if only that were true
for us here.

Father & Son Q&A

co-authored by Nikola S. Pesich and Robert S. Pesich

When will you melt down
the greased mousetraps on your nightstand?

But you did not answer, when the night sky burns, why do you follow?

Is there anyone in the house
that can pronounce your name?

Remember, it is still important to ask why
do we need to touch when we now breathe
through our devices.

Ok. Then we might make millions
opening a Nothing-Stand.

What if I apprentice myself to the wind?

Remember your name, both miracle and wound.

Blasphemous Pilgrim

It is not enough to know
that there are cypresses leaning
over the cliffs into their continual births.

Nor is it enough to know
how to build Neruda's boat
out of burning matches and newspaper.

How to ply silences with unanswered questions,
with color photos of the emptiness,
to a horizon of black and white

under an unabridged edition of sky.

May the wind teach me how to write
the first word of your breath tonight,
shape of sea and river entering each other

accompanied by the cries of the terns
announcing the continual arrival of a pilgrim
clothed in scabs and dreams

in your chapel of moonlight
the sound of your voice in the breaking waves
setting my idols ablaze.

Kitchen Science No. 7: Surface Tension

Bring me a sharp sewing needle,
a spool of silk thread,
tissues, to handle the riddle.
No. Instead of thread

please, cut one dark strand of your hair
long as our newborn.
Now, pour nine cups of cold water
into this basin.

Threaded, lay it on the clear skin
cradled in tissues,
steel tied to time, dream, a question.
They float before us

working our depths, the silences.
Grab and they plunge straight through your wounds.

The 6 O'Clock Commute

How long must one lean upon nothing
in order to live within lightning?

What happens to our name
when there is no falling or flying
only standing in line?

Tissue Culture

Some hearts dissolve in one day.
Their many families of cells live on
inside incubators. Myocytes
growing in petri dishes through winter.
Invisible scaffolding guides their migrations,
nomads searching once again for each other.
They do not forget where they come from.
When they meet, they join,
beating in unison.

The student checks their pulse
at noon and at midnight,
notes changes in morphology,
new cell-cell contacts.
He does not notice
the sugar ant
dragging a black hair
into the crack in the floor.
Who knows how far back down.

Food for the Queen.
Or maybe digested into glue
to plug a growing void in the wall.
Or to tie our breath
to the other side of the wind.

Chinese Lanterns in a Shadowbox

>   Inspired by Previously New, mixed media
>   —Lynn Powers

Dried vasculatures
wrapped around red seeds
or maybe just rot
not unlike some premises
that dare us to touch
while the splinter waits in the frame
knowing more about the knife,
the brush, the pen
how the invisible lives.

The Envelope Has Something to Say

Fine. Pick your teeth with the edge of my face.
But if you scribble on my back
the names of your devils
and then ignore them?

Don't think your voice is always delivered.
Sometimes, I prefer to read your silences.

You're not going to burn me if I continue?
Who says there are no white cranes in this city
when I can feel them waking in your hands.

Within my four corners, an edge of your face
disappearing into the horizon
in search of a passage
to the New World.

From a Dead Fox in a Suburban Backyard

Do not forget
to address your letter to the absences,
your questions concerning the sky

and the mountain's destination as it disappears
along with the blue songs
that nest in your nights.

And will I continue to nurse
the silvery nerve of the earth
conducting the first and last

syllable of your name?
To find the silences in there
is to glimpse the falcon in flight

only a few know how to follow
as it collects every angle of emptiness
in order to pull out of its dive

while in an instant, the voice of your infant
gone. Your own breath
broken at both ends.

Algorithm, this suturing and tearing.
Do not bury me in a world of less and less.
Wind and sun will wash me

will dissolve the last scent of milk,
will scatter us into the voices of others.

ACKNOWLEDGEMENTS

Grateful acknowledgment is made to the editors of the following publications and anthologies in which these poems or earlier versions previously appeared:

Albatross: "Mice and other guests"

And We The Creatures: "Pet Shop"

Aperçus Quarterly: "Total Lunar Eclipse" and "The *eyeless* gene in *Drosophila melanogaster*"

The Bitter Oleander: "A Few Questions," "And what will you admit," "Blasphemous pilgrim," "From a dead fox in a suburban backyard," "Tissue Culture," "Kitchen Science No. 7: Surface Tension," and "The 6 O'Clock Commute"

Mediphors: "Cardiac Morphogenesis"

Porter Gulch Review: "A Quick Stop at the Natural Life Aquarium," "Recommendation: maggot therapy for wound debridement"

Red Wheelbarrow: "Dressing Up in Down Times" and "*Xenopus laevis*: African Clawed Frog"

Riverbabble: "Chinese lanterns in a shadowbox"

Sand Hill Review: "The Stomach"

Santa Clara Review: "To a Red-Tailed Hawk"

Sleet Magazine: "Heart Massage"

Skidrow Penthouse: "Scar" and "The envelope has something to say"

The Montserrat Review: "A Window in the City"

The Redwood Coast Review: "Production of the Next, Safe Happies"

I would also like to thank the following institutions whose support was invaluable to me as I wrote these poems: Djerassi Resident Artists Program, Silicon Valley Community Foundation Fellowship, Silicon Valley Creates and Villa Montalvo Arts Center.

www.ingramcontent.com/pod-product-compliance
Lightning Source LLC
Chambersburg PA
CBHW071758080526
44588CB00013B/2289